The Look of Goodbye

Peter Robinson was born in Salford, Lancashire, in 1953 and grew up mainly in Liverpool. He has degrees from the universities of York and Cambridge. After eighteen years teaching in Japan, he is now professor of English and American literature at the University of Reading. The author of many books of poetry, prose, translations, and literary criticism, he is married and the father of two daughters.

By the Same Author

Poetry

Overdrawn Account
Anaglypta
This Other Life
More About the Weather
Entertaining Fates
Leaf-Viewing
Lost and Found
Via Sauro Variations
Anywhere You Like
About Time Too
Selected Poems
There are Avenues
Ghost Characters

Prose

Untitled Deeds

Interviews

Talk about Poetry: Conversations on the Art

Translations

Six Poems by Ungaretti
The Great Friend and Other Translated Poems
The Greener Meadow: Selected Poems of Luciano Erba
Selected Poetry and Prose of Vittorio Sereni

Criticism

In the Circumstances: About Poems and Poets
Poetry, Poets, Readers: Making Things Happen
Twentieth Century Poetry: Selves and Situations

PETER ROBINSON

THE LOOK OF GOODBYE

Poems 2001-2006

Shearsman Books
Exeter

Published in the United Kingdom in 2008 by
Shearsman Books Ltd
58 Velwell Road
Exeter EX4 4LD

ISBN 978-1-905700-45-5

Contents

One

Two

Three

Four

Five

Six

for Ornella, Matilde & Giulia

One

The Red Dusk

for Paul Lally

I'm starting from the teddy-choirboy
who taught us what painting the town red meant
in a city where you simply had to know
who'd done what on any given Saturday
at Anfield or away —
where lives would be one long might-have-been
if the referee was blind or a linesman biased;
and even though you'll never walk alone
I could almost taste it in a smoky sky
welling up like burst blood-vessels round the gates,
full time blown, as down we went
with the rivers of red between brick terrace houses.

You remember: a sunset was blazing on the Mersey
where the battleship *Potemkin* — let's say — lay
at anchor through the policemen's strike . . .
Uplifted, carried forward by a dimmed red tide,
red-nosed, red-faced, we were each being sent
off into the late light of a vast inflamed eye.

Brief Visitation

You again, and even here
back-lit against the window pane,
it's as if you bring me
word of a possible way to be,
of things I could only say with you listening,
things that don't have sense without you —
like a gleam coming in through the window,
its light reflected off piled snow.

Yes, and I'm astonished by
you again, you in this room here with me
(perhaps you're shrugging, shaking your head
at every least thing I've said)
or else I'm listening, lost for words,
and eyes un-focus on a pattern-less carpet,
you saying, 'Don't fret, don't forget . . .'
out of the blue bright sky.

You again, and even here
the pine trees' stiffened waves of ice
look pleased to be noticed by one more stranger.
Defunct firms, bars, non-places impinge or
defer for a moment to this bitter afternoon
when, sooner or later, go you must —
and you're leaving very, very soon,
you again, if only just.

Alien Registration

'Dr. Robinson, you need to renew
your alienation card . . .'

Daybreak and even the clouds flake
away at their edges like fish scales,
like rust, like blood on your lenses.
For a moment, I'm really not sure
where this particular darkness visible
might be, and you know how it is, an obscure
remorse or worse, something worse
sticks round the memories of words;
and I squirm as between clock and bed,
porous with daylight, darker shapes
fill out the outline in a vanity mirror
speckled at its edges; and sure enough,
glancing at the photograph,
you notice a face they no longer recognize.

So you know, you don't need to be told
how the frustrations will gather
at a stuck traffic signal or stop-sign,
when queues in official places
leave us all at another loose end . . .
There'll be little else for it but to take
that gap between sky and unfenced concrete
as storm clouds come sloping above me
to shed their droplets on the finest grey
dust you might ever hate to see —
being humbled by that disintegrating day
when any slight change in the weather
was enough to be wondering what in the world
could possibly put it back together?

As Like as Not

'Is the Pacific Sea my home?
John Donne

Comes an ambivalent sky towards evening,
dark dropping fast as we climb
up through the higgledy-piggledy houses
with dusk-flares in overgrown
blind corner mirrors, precarious
contracts, un-renewable futures
reflected as street-fronts and shop-fronts aglow
back here in the back of beyond
where it's like our real life were over:
we're living a posthumous existence,
a paradise or purgatory, whatever,
picked out like the ant platoons
at work on a hillside of caves,
their cunning passages in the glooms
under hortensia leaves.

And this is what's become of us.
Endangered, we have lived
playing noughts and crosses with the days
squared out on a calendar;
we've coped with the solitude,
the postal disappointments or delays,
chewing seaward cloud
and other enigmatic food.

Past rows of gingko or zelkova, elm,
we've tried to seem at home,
though now and again I'm overwhelmed
by neon in late afternoon, an alien
gazing at an alien horizon.

Then yet once more, in this far-off sunset,
I'll start on a theme to reconcile
ourselves with precipitous mountains
and the benefits of exile.

Transit Lounge

1

Now as that story's stopped meaning a thing
and the next one not barely begun,
when neither here nor there we're over
the Gulf of Finland or Baltic, it might be
you find yourself over-susceptibly
sustained by no more than a song,
moved by implausibly lucky plot twists
bringing tears with no sense to the eye.
It might be, as like, you discover
hopes and regrets I thought we were over
catching up in the cloudless sky;
then subside, exhausted, barely exist
in that thin red arc across a map
somewhere on the edge of sleep —
till awoken for our continental breakfast.

2

Then it might be this place we've arrived at
so as to leave it shows promise
of futures not ours in the distance,
a distance with church spires, with fir trees
and no choices, nothing else for it
but the fire crews' practice wrecks
parked like *memento mori* on an apron —
us sitting, waiting, watching the spray
from long-haul carriers as they touch down.

3

Nothing else for it since we don't want
soft toys, souvenirs, or the duty free,
don't want to thin attenuated
senses of selfhood, despise others' children

at their games of hide-and-seek
circling around us with shrill cries —
but squirm from them as all I've hated
finds me out here in my weakness,
here in the limbo of now.

4

Though now I've my feet on the ground,
the ground slightly rises and falls
with an undulant motion, it seems.
Then we wrap ourselves up in the tiredness,
ineluctable circumstance, and slow time
of a day going on far too long.

5

Long drawn out by this three-hour loose end,
we even get used to the transit lounge —
being nowhere in particular
with time to kill or spare,
and specially when the sky
starts to prepare for its night-flight schedules,
when thoughts of being or getting there
are beaten to airy thinness by
streams of blood in the layered cloud cover —
we even get used to this being for now
among thousands of the other stranded souls.

For the Birds

for Ralph and Hester

Certainly, rare birds converged on your lawn
one summer's day as from the east,
north, round the corner they had flown

in for a chat, yes, and what a commotion
that parakeet on upper branches caused —
and what quiet once they're gone.

Raubkunst

It would have been better to ask permission
before stealing a glimpse of suburbs
on Vienna's furthest outskirts with the woods,
and woodland paths for taking a stroll
one autumn afternoon, my words
taken into quiet air but still not quite
enough coming back to set me at my ease —
which is why there was yet more to tell
like a confession, a therapy session,
though no one would be paid for the time
and as if it were making the slightest difference
to dead wood crackling underfoot,
the creak in high branches, a rummaging breeze
that stirred perpetually tops of trees . . .
It would have been better to ask permission.

Poplar, walnut, birch, diseased
chestnut leaves are motionless
and, for garden statuary,
take this draped, reclining figure
held up by two wicker chairs
who's talking to me here.

But caught up in an over-crowded dream
like the thick mist filling sunlit fields
from Innsbruck to Salzburg, its luminous gleam
populous with things you were to see
in moments intervening, I hear him say,
'Now we're all for the freedom of art
in its own time, though painted with opprobrium,
become common property,' and I'm
not even missing the closed Belvedere,
its glimpses of expropriated Klimts
with their gilt frames, gold showers, touched-up displays

like drowned lives that flashed before the eyes
of gallery-goers moving through silence
filled with the dispossessed, burned, the lost.

Equally ours, more ideas
start as conversations slow,
framing landscapes for the ears
in a light of near departure —
although there's barely a shadow
of that cast on each feature;

and perspectives extend beyond the garden
to take in flea markets, maples, a shrine
with misunderstandings or taken offence,
as at those earlier attempts of mine —
bunglings not supposed to happen
that did, the more-than-bargained-for
lingering still in every consequence
like visits unmade, a fast stain from the things
you didn't do or, done, you can't undo.
But now the mown lawn's taken an imprint;
train timetables must play their part,
hushed leaves stirring memories to the last.
Taking my leave . . . he saw what I meant.
It would have been better to ask permission
before stealing away with that past.

Bohemia-on-Sea

Out walking made those small streets your own
with buddleia, ivy, privet, rhododendron,
bindweed, laburnum, all the various words
salted away for a time afterwards
when spawned frogs swarming in a garden pond
would form a metropolis, I'm to understand,
a bohemia which you map for me
by pointing to docklands, telling a story
of rises and falls, some harpy or lout
who loses, who wins, who's in, who's out,
and take upon us the mystery of things . . .
being counted among such poor beings
already at an age of resigned retrospect.
Still, not so far off, the would-be elect
swarm on each other's backs, leave us alone
to lock-up garages, park lakes, the blue plaques made your own.

Inside his gallery flat, I start
to sense the claustrophobia
of still life objects, a still warm heart
straitening itself to be here;
and surrounded by the things you want,
hear art's latest candidate
small talk each opposite house-front
about the ins and outs of it.

Looked at in that light, it's already evening
and late again for whatever this might be,
under the low cloud ceiling, I hurry
down a corridor of stationary cars,
dodge the street furniture's bins or bollards,
then half-obscured by a porch lamp, pause
with familiar uncertainty and words
on the tip of my tongue, here, at a threshold,
one hand reaching towards the front door's
bell push, readying myself to say sorry.

A Tribute

About a train journey over the border,
I'm finding it harder
and harder to put out of mind or explain
why, when I came from a cramped waiting room,
a young girl or, rather, young woman
had me rooted to the platform —
for it wasn't as if, after all, I knew
or had ever set eyes on her before.
Perhaps because her thick fall of red hair
threw me back off down the years
to a towpath where I'm racking my brains
for a word to say as minute by minute
our time's made a series of tortures
(her silence, mine) and me like
one of those hapless government spokesmen
who's no sooner opened his mouth
than he puts a foot in it . . .

which was when the journey began in earnest.
Through seeming-deserted country, our train
at its new speed limit racketed on
across yet more debatable terrain —
everywhere owned and abandoned
even by trespassing walkers, depressed
farmers, their eyes
streaming at fumes from ministry fires
behind a horizon, crooked smoke plumes
meeting the cloud-base above livestock pyres
like a tribute to the gods of brand and
profit; through hill fields, healthy areas
where the rest of flocks still safely graze,
we're sent down false tracks till with house roofs
on Lockerbie's outskirts, it slowed again
by heaps of heifers' blackened hooves
pointing at the skies.

Totes Meer

Here they dismantled the bulging defences
to pre-empt their fall and then found
earlier eras of wall left behind.

Now the defences' graveyard, like a sea,
is these grey slabs laid end to end
in a drained marsh, every numbered stone
glistening from the clouded night's rain.

I'm stopped by a bit of parapet
(its memorial plaque long since ripped away)
relieving myself, and the steaming pee
fountains into that tufted reed bed
paved with hand-carved anonymous tombs
like a sea, like a petrified sea.

Babel Tower

Languishing languages, dying dialects
bereft of mouths and ears
with barely anyone left to sound them,
let alone poets who can make them sing . . .

It's like you'd already forgotten
sunsets reflected on a thousand windows,
forgotten each monosyllabic cry
of construction workers ensconced in the sky
where scaffolding grids cross-hatch heaped cloud
overwrought with the colourful meaning.

It's like you'd already forgotten
love-scribbles in steamed-up panes or dust,
your senses, the feeling made known,
then lost with every unnamed thing.

Perhaps, perhaps you hardly knew
more than a garbled bird-call
as pidgin-idiom warbles interrupt
empty blue silence, then nothing at all.

Now, even now, Babel Tower's to be kept up.

After Words

Like a late January truce,
an end to the winter's contention
or, alright, a temporary one,
today, this clear sky's disappeared sun
glowing up from a mountain horizon
as it ends these luminous hours has no use;
but, still, it's being used
by reflective plate-glass street fronts,
clouds progressing across them;
and because I've no quarrel with the badly-abused
landscape as such —
its red-and-white-striped chimneys
dispersing traces of smoke,
no quarrel at all with flaked sunshine
speckling miles of tiled roofs and the like
down to a broad ocean skyline,
the tenuous branches of serpentine trees
with cotton-wool flocks still behind them,
it's like the visible world had reopened,
refurbishments complete,
and most of it thankfully wordless —
if you'll allow me to admit that much.

Numbers Game

1

Approaching the ancestral tombs
in their stands of pine,
I'm wondering how many mildewed stone stairs
there are here, how many years
it is since last I climbed them,
and hear myself learning to count, once again,
on flights of worn-down steps
as we make our way back to the grandparents' house
at 22 Sea View Terrace
however many years ago.

2

Now groves are stillness itself on the climb.
By black iron railings and a children's graveyard
I've misjudged the time.

It's past 4:30 and that gentler slope
towards the ancestral tomb museum,
my short cut's just been closed.

3

Damp shadows, red pine bark, the hollowed-out stone,
flowerless peonies, silence and moss
pass as I practise the rule of adding one . . .

When they asked me how many home, back then,
I could hardly guess.

4

Approaching the ancestral tombs
in their stands of pine,
I've had to take a long way round

5

and keep on over the cared-for ground
wondering why it should be
that though numbers came, you still can't know
how many years more or less there are,
how many stairs to climb
before you arrive near the top, the top
step, step up and go.

Planetarium

Drifting off into the Milky Way,
the darkness of a tired brain
and this false night sky confused,
you don't know if stars
are confetti thrown over our heads again
or memories at the edge of sleep,
don't know whether Zodiac signs
were written on our firmament like fates
or read into the time it takes
for matter to travel across
space and mind, and so be gone —
time, after all, being only that motion.

Whichever it is, you're at a loss
adrift with the music of the spheres
as various hoary tales
like Rorschach blot or eye-test card
signal across interstellar tracts
of mental conflict, galactic wars.
The talk-over's a lullaby you hear
tell of labyrinths, distances
where creatures blink then disappear.
Whichever it is, adrift you try
to concentrate on them and know
your place among the stars.

To that Effect

Loneliness, it's like furniture.
As if planed wood held memories
of wind hauling leaves from all the world's trees,
your room may be full but, sure
enough, like holes in a piece of cheese
left to sweat on the kitchen table,
loneliness, it's like furniture.
They're both uncountable.

The Better Halves

'The secret of survival in a place like
Sendai was clearly self-effacement . . .'
Robert Fraser

One cold winter Sunday morning
at the main hall of a Buddhist temple complex
our local Italo-Japan Association
is calling down good fortune with its prayers
for the likes of Buffon, Maldini, Cannavaro . . .
players from the national team
due here during their World Cup competition.
Televised, our wives throw handfuls of beans
for the occasion, in the event,
throw ceremonial tangerines
towards those believers' raised arms.

Meanwhile, in a late morning's pallid grey,
I'm at the non-event of a five-tier
pagoda undergoing restoration,
gazing at the impact, the fact of it —
that scaffolding box with polythene sheet
soundless in a lack of any breeze.
I'm here on this non-occasion by a brazier,
a heat-contorted box of iron mesh
giving off heat, still filled with red-hot ash,
white plumes coughed out while they burn bric-a-brac
of remembrance, effigies and charms
that were to bring good fortune to last year.

And I warm myself at it as they all go up in smoke;
and I wait for our wives to reappear.

Two

Closure

In another town you turn a corner,
but it's not there any more —
the place with hunting pieces, flagons,
a close-hung mish-mash of daubs and prints.

Here clean breasts were made, minds spoken —
our waiter boning fish, all
genial, patient, hardly bothered
if once more we prove the last to leave.

*

But dust has gathered
on lintel and sill.
Restoration work this morning's
at a standstill . . .

I squint through smeared windows,
see greyness, a grey
of no menus, mementos,
no things.

*

And I see how the vacant ex-restaurant
through its cloud of chalk
is like nothing so much as a sea shell
in which you catch talk
that talked and went so far with distant
wave-forms broken on the shore
of others' minds like swell, swell
echoing from the years before.

The False Perspectives

Everything's sloping off anywhere else —
like that faulty landscape
with a crack in it, a gap.
Down there, whatever the false
perspectives carrying us away,
they also serve
to bring back, just once in a while, a love
along with the whole cabaret
of mental furniture, double acts, turns,
rare views from the provinces . . .
and love, she makes her entrances,
exits under your defences
where everything sloping off returns.

Where larger items in the distance
grow to insignificance
as they go near, I'm done
explaining to her mother —
nothing untoward between us, no one
proved wrong or right, but rather
spaces weakening the ties
and all of it like a sleight-of-mind
deceiving us, while eyes
follow a stream to the hill's brow,
or I'm leaning from a window
to touch the paths that wind
there, there which used to be where here is now.

Mi último adiós

My last goodbye to an imaginary love
began with an earful from some irate neighbour.
I'd rung the wrong bell for the flat above
set in London brick beside your door.

Visibly shaken, I should have known before;
but here you were as good as saying
there wouldn't be a space my size any more
in the journal of your going or staying.

As day slid by, sun moved round attic windows.
Likewise, it couldn't be long before you went
westward and out beyond the Andes —
as I would as soon to my Orient.

York Notes

1

Just you wait, you wait and see
how the landscaping matures!
That gaggle of graylag geese
are stopping traffic at Foss Island,
their critical mass a menace
to grass verges, flagstones, cars.

2

Remembered words for a would-be love
about the lake, a bridge and reeds
being far too Japanese
turn out quite true enough —
what with the language spoken
by those two in cahoots
under weeping willow trees.

3

Those kids chase ducks and coots
across an old hall's lawn . . .
Yes, how the landscaping matures
until you hardly recognize
your self, it is so overgrown.

Languages of Weather

For a momentary feeling of changed
idiom in an atmosphere,
I'm listening through static, white noise,
through the chores and challenged
dutiful attempts to be here;
I listen for the sound of a voice
as for a passing, brief sensation
in the languages of weather,
something that might have been sensed by
a relative or someone
at the corner of a street, the sky.

Tired, its pitch contour flattens
as on a cardiac monitor,
flat vowels a perpetual surprise
to somebody muffled in headphones
hearing the intonation patterns
of a voice I barely recognize,
known as it sounds through the bones,
one lost and found then lost again
with a serial forgetfulness,
a mirror, clothes hanger, and pen.

'Speak for yourself,' I hear it say —
like slant light piercing an overcast day.

White Lines

Take, if you like, the green woodpecker
at work on bark of a poplar tree:
its stubborn, red-crested action brings
far echoes with each tell-tale knock
tap-tapping through thick traffic back to us
in a breakfast table air . . .

Take tendrils drawn from an ivy wall,
or that heron at the torrent's brink
keeping its feet wet as we bike by
in a day of forms and hurried talk,
faxes, photocopies, sad or sorry queues . . .
Yet somehow still I hear myself think
despite the brief cicadas' racket,
the Vespas, programmes, ephemeral news . . .

Like cumulo-nimbus in a sunset,
late on some horizon, doubts arise
with, capping it all, the summer lightning,
its remote, mute detonations
flashed across cloud-cupolas and domes.
No, you don't hear a thing.

The arrowed forks and flare-flames
strike like so many un-sourced quotations
escaped from the lost deads' un-thumbed tomes;
but because they can't remember us,
resentful, we've forgotten them —
and an obscure grief or shamefulness
forms from dark by the road's white lines,
among allusive adverts and clear signs.

Real Times

For the man on a park bench reading his paper,
appearing entirely absorbed
in headlines, adverts, gossip, sport,
the wood slats of his seat are no less hard;
and really there's no disputing whether
he's grateful for the shade
on this August afternoon —
we're all connoisseurs of shadow here.

Children are swinging on a bald car tyre
whose heaviness is evident;
and so their parents intervene
helping them go higher.
We listen and respond in real time
to a line of talk about memory
or the sense like self-betrayal
of not being able to wish somebody well.

True, we go back a long way.
The river walk swarmed with greenfly
on that blame-filled day.
It turned out they were Judas trees.
I saw mist on the train yards.
So all these things became you
as you grew shy, more shy,
like smoke from near chimneys.

Equally, the crackle of each turned-over page
set off by an apple bough
has me reading myself with dismay.
Fresh problems diagnosed from the data,
I'm responding to them now
even if they'll be reprocessed later
in the diurnal give-and-take
of however long the given takes to say.

Stranded

for Peter Swaab

No shortage of footprints in the sand,
boats aplenty on a sea horizon,
and after ages spent under an umbrella
trying to remain in the shade,
I couldn't be less like a Robinson Crusoe
wretchedly lonely for his humankind.

Man Friday sells sun-hats to savages,
the bronzed, scanning action and equity;
Suzanne comes offering massages;
but I stare off into the great sky gulf
out of love with all humanity
starting from myself . . .

Still here the station looks over that sea
horizon at sunset, its line interrupted
by shrubs, oleanders in flower,
white lamps aglow for the dusk and all this
niched into a cliff-face with two tunnel mouths
opened at either end.

The station's like a tended shrine
with bougainvillea to distract me
from timetable nerves, and a full moon
blurred above neon, pantographs, sea,
being gazed at by home-bound bathers
ready to doze off along their line.

The station is a stretch of brightness
growing shadowed between
dark gulfs, even now, as a train

breaks up this respite's last light and place
with its dead weight, its braking force,
and crowded coaches are gone from what was

the most beautiful station you'd ever seen.

What Lies Sleeping

Then it comes out with the sight of faint breeze
that billows a sun-filled lace curtain
like serried phantom pregnancies,
the abstracted gaze
of a woman who suddenly loses her looks
in childbirth, or of eyes
disappointed in marriage whose tears
start as if unbidden
at something somebody says . . .

which is how unutterable meaning
makes itself felt now a loved one
nods off on the train
as features are shedding defences
to tired eyes or, again,
a life's glimpsed with no stances,
without self-presentation —
this truth never hidden from the senses;
it just needed underlining.

High Time

1

Brained by fronds and branches, crowned
with leafage slipped down over the eyes,
that's how I stumble on this empty beach round midday,
aware of the other ones bending away
beyond headlands, and how these
histories of slow swell lapping on shorelines
make themselves felt as so many mild concussions,
numberless whisperings to a tired mind,
and how at sea defences, harbour wall or bay
smelling an air of fish-work and wrack
I follow the paths by gleaming black anchors,
nets, the floats, and hear dogs bark —
there being that many ways to feel confined.

2

So as the ocean mitigates silences
and waves flash with daylight piercing through cloud tails,
we're in an in-between chasing our children,
the summer still ending without a finale;
and that's why I wander all down the shoreline,
jetsam and driftwood dried in the sun,
and why, understanding how it's not possible,
count starfish or flotsam, accepting acceptance,
given alternatives, there being none.

3

And I gaze round the shoreline
at a busy sky's action,
the rough curve of shell-shards
forming its tide mark, your words
backed up by delight and fear
in our two girls' cries.

4

High time, it's time the sights of these
cormorant sentinels up on a cliff
from a pleasure craft in calmer seas,
or that gull's wing flexing above
raised fingers, its red-tipped beak, its eyes
trained towards food the children leave
on ripple and wave were examples of . . .
High time, even if I don't say it enough.

Silence Revisited

'What silence
penetrating rock
the voice of the cicada'

Matsuo Bashō

After the gauntlet of parking attendants,
present vendors, signs
any tourist trap wants,
one early May we were making that climb
again up a cliff-front
with pauses and vertigo
at breath-taking stone steps, outcrops, viewing platforms
precarious on narrow, high ledges.

From here I look down to the hills'
profiles in a haze;
for, yes, there was mist across valleys this time
all seen without alien
sensations of years ago,
with no ten years' bickerings, sulks or resentments,
tit-for-tats, cries . . .
In the silence, I was wondering where they had gone.

Here again, the eyes have it; they're ravished
by ivy inching on a wall,
the azaleas' moment under bruised skies,
and because by temple plots
I was tempted still to pick a quarrel
but thought better of it,
(as if sounds had all been absorbed into the rock)
it seemed that what the landscape wanted
was only for us to rise above it.

Unwitting Epitaph

But all too soon they had to be off.
He thanked us warmly for the evening,
a gentle architect whose laugh
was catching, and we caught it,
even though I thought our children
might have overdone the joke
and said so, just as they were leaving,
'Come along now, that's enough.'

Three

Taking Off

for Katy Price

1

It wasn't long after the plane took off
on its twelve-hour haul to Paris
when word cut in through the cabin intercom.
'If there's a doctor or nurse on board
will they please come forward,' our purser said,
and make themselves known to a member of the crew.'
But then that was the last we heard.
The flight went on with its usual routine.
Over roadsteads, enclaves, field-systems we flew
as west Siberian lowlands gave way
to cloud convoys of a Baltic day . . .

2

It was only at the end we knew.
There were procedures the Paris police
had to go through perforce.
Because everyone of us had taken off
but he never landed, we couldn't disembark.
Yes, I know there's no kidding with the dead.
Soon, though, we'd put on our shades and walk
from an exit of that makeshift flying hearse.

Italian Poplars

We live in thin air sold off by a villa
up on the top floor where birds would soar or dive,
screened by one flank of a tree-lined drive.
Its poplar leaves quiver though the branches are still.
Beyond them, suggestions of windows, a doorway
with lamp lit above it in the gloaming you see.
Then yellow, a risen August moon gone astray
startles, complete, above surrounding greenery.
It's as if I'd invited that full moon in our bedroom
and in spite of these mosquito screens it came
filling the new house with a quieter light —
while you, quite naked in the French window frame,
silhouetted on a wall's late-modern, matt white,
had seduced the uncanny, being home.

Mentioned in Dispatches

i.m. F. T. Prince

So there we are outside a fish and chip shop
'with a streak of red that might have issued from Christ's breast'
where the river meets the sky
and rain coming on, a suggestion of rain.

And there we are running for his car
when our veteran of the Italian campaign
(who it seems may have been among Captain Prince's soldiers
bathing in that respite from the Second World War)
trips on a curb and goes thump on a flagstone
to the sound of a seagull's mocking cry.

And I know it could happen to anyone
but this is our lance-corporal who has fallen,
our interpreter of captured Wehrmacht maps.
And I'm, like, looming over him
like a younger generation to tread him down
when I see he's hurt, he's in some pain
(who bivouacked on Monte Cassino's slopes
et in arcadia survived the jaundice and malaria).

But his number's not up, he's not gone for a Burton;
and we help him back onto his feet again.

The Found Voice

Someone, the day before yesterday,
as like as not a relative,
stood in that bay window niche
trying his level best to give
voice to a life-long bitterness
about an outside loo and one cold tap . . .

who suddenly turned to a little lad watching
lorries and dray horses pass
from the whitened stone front step
of Tasker's hot pie shop
in Portman Street, Manchester,
around the time of the Wall Street Crash.

I knew that outside toilet and cold tap,
would go to do my business
on afternoons we paid a visit;
but couldn't find one single trace
of hurt remembering the Rusholme house.
For me their poverty was no disgrace

and yet, it's true, I found a voice
in abundant curiosity
about what he'd abandoned
with no wish to break years' silences,
or mention that stone step in the city
where he would sit and play —

till, that is, the day before yesterday.

Platt Fields

Some time after those Indian Jewellers'
in what becomes the Wilmslow Road
appeared a space of open greenness
with slender, beseeching winter trees;
and I remembered passing by
dark iron railings that capped a low wall
as if it were a cemetery
with my granddad buried inside.
In fact, he'd been cremated,
his ashes at rest I don't know where.
Still, what a curious place contained him —
far distances to tennis courts
and between tree trunks, in my imagination;
but I could only glimpse it,
Elysian, glancing from that bus
or friend of the family's car back then.
It comes just after Claremont Road
has branched off to the right.
Nothing remains of my grandparents' house,
the puddled crack where we might play
or long route dad, a choir boy,
would take to Holy Trinity, Platt.
Then what was it supposed to mean
if not that the life of streets has an end,
yet something else stretches beyond?

March 1993

Hope Hospital

for my parents

It was one of those mild days towards winter's end
when a sun's lengthy shadow makes you think
of what the weather might have been back then.

I'm laid on my spine here gazing from the pram
into a blue and white, cloud-tracked sky
this fine March day more than fifty years ago.

As sunshine changes, clouds arrive or leave,
being part of earth's vast annual routine,
they signal to your first-born that he is alive.

So, yes, you could surely wonder how and why
this kind of thing began, if it began
here on the front path at 10 Duffield Road

with infinite varieties of light effect, of line
that take me back, take me aback . . . and yet
those quiet hours where 'Hope' would 'Objects find',

weren't they exactly what I'm destined to forget?

Life is Good

after Martin Vincent

One muggy day in summer time
with the cityscape at sunset
and a new-age tramway station
silhouetted against late-coloured sky,
what you've got to smile about
stranded on another platform
caused by points failure . . . caused by
whatever it was when it's at home,
I haven't the faintest idea.

But then you don't go into that;
you number streaks on brickwork
of cotton mill conversions,
canal marina, sunlit windows'
dusky clouds distended,
or steeples, with an expert's
eye for further hillsides,
a season's close-packed greenery
between the precincts, crescents' shops,
all the swarming enclaves
of a suburb's outskirts —

while I have people waiting for me,
no signals change, and someone
wanders up the snaking lines
past sleepers, by infested sidings.
The public address, just interference,
mauls excuse or explanation
as fellow-travellers, marooned,
exchange an understanding glance;
and still your genial irony
manages blankly to outface
any number of such mishaps.

Good for you, and my lookout,
now the orange signalman
climbs back to his whitewashed box.
Two coaches crawl across the section.
You smile, and put it down to fate.
Still fretting over the collapse
of arrangements to be met,
I miss the comic side . . . ah but . . .
that's like a debt to my own nature,
family background, Manchester,
chalked up on the slate.

Calm Autumn

'Stretched out on the floor,
ear to a short-wave radio,
we were bent to hear
would it be peace or war?'

After the traumas, storms and disappointments
sometimes an autumnal calm
day, like this one, comes as if in recompense;
yes and at moments like this one,
lucky, it's all I can do to enjoy
a strobe-effect of sunlight through the high,
anti-suicide fence's bars
as I take the same old bridge across that gorge.

There's a lurid yellow glow above the sea;
there are stark factory
smoke-stacks standing out against it.
Then flashed off the estuary
are similar tints like a boy with a mirror, sky
still showing its complement of hawks,
and again that interrupted sun
signals like an echo of the ships within far gulfs.

★

You see the line of national flags
at a sports day's end when somebody drags it
through grey dust.
                    I'm put out by swags
strung across roof-space in a gym —
then think again now rows of them
hang limp above the Luna-Park
in a post-dusk, a first dark.

★

And yet once more I'm dealing
with thoughts of us stretched out on a mat floor
in another seaport, feeling
nausea come like the breakers at its groyne —
heard too in our shore hotel;
ear to a short-wave radio,
through the crackle of static we were trying to tell
would it be peace or war . . .

        ★

It would be war; but now these twelve years later
we see-saw in a rhythm with the days
while leaves are cascading from branches in utter
confusion, strewn over avenues and drives,
are clawed at like the last rags on frayed trees;
and, as when a cartoon character
steps inadvertently out above a drop,
from nowhere somebody among us says —

Don't look, but we're having the time of our lives.

My Italy

'Pace, pace, pace. —'
  Francesco Petrarca

When the balconies blossomed with identical banners
all the colours of a rainbow coalition
in suburbs we wandered around street corners
where house-fronts were forming an apt quotation.

And though the peace party would inevitably lose,
I wasn't inclined to fix tired eyes
on anything else than flags like those —
that one word printed on them more than headline-size.

So we followed the parallels of apartment balconies
bedecked with allusions to a poet's words
in earliest springtime while flowering magnolias,

cherry trees by sidings, and sound-bites of birds
were also just responses to our long-prolonged cries
from the states' and petty tyrants' perpetual wars.

Parma, 22 March 2003

Naturally Enough

Caught out in a storm again
after all these years,
I'm not trying to be struck by
anything, making repairs,
repairing from the rain
when even the heavens seem on a war footing,
light crepitating through leaves.
With thunder runs, the sky
unburdens itself and I think it grieves
for whatever drive-by shooting,
intelligence failure, executive crime
or discriminate murder
has likely been done in its name.

Sheltering near an out-of-order
Cola machine, that moth
in camouflage kit lies playing dead —
unless, unless it's died.
A beetle flees the downpour
fording gutters turned to floods,
and I'm identified
with a rush of cool wind through these woods
like an antique
sensation, a throwback
to electrical discharges flared in a face
or hair stood on end
by the ionized air.
Sheeting rain pockmarks the surface
of mediterranean rain-pools and rattles
a bike shed's corrugated iron,
and I try to repair
when even the elements seem at war.

Enduring Peace

One of those mornings when the whole world's cast
looks like another black mark against us,
when even the gravel noise gets on your nerves
and early bell-tolls start a thought,
I take my familiar walk to work
through a temple precinct that kind of preserves
how peace used to be.

Now, now it's like we're all shell-shocked,
shell-shocked at one remove
and battle fatigued through an ever after
of post traumatic stress disorder
started by back-firing cars;
we're enduring a state of war-like peace,
or peace like war.

From dimmed reflections in a subway train window
there comes yet one more
grim reminder, a smashed face blurred
by speed and the weakness of your strained eyes . . .

Now, now at tunnel mouths, racketing forward,
that's when our dreadfully sorry spectacle,
when this whole world takes on the view
of how quite other peace could be

preserved, or kind of, from the years before.

English Abroad

See here, this far from home, odd
characters with their English greeting,
a fleeting eye contact or minimal nod.
It's the sign of compatriots meeting
who'd like to commiserate, but
the language just rummages inside them
as if it were fretting to find a way out . . .
Still down the neon-flecked avenue some
word sticks in your throat
or dies on wintry wind-chapped lips.
You bear it in mind, like a scar, and that note
echoes the more perhaps.

The Quick Way

for Stephen Romer

From those only too suitable cups of tea
to a required *Monoprix*
we stepped into a church on Rue Saint-Antoine,
pretty sure it was the one
that led back to a bookshop in Rue Charles V.
Past tearful Madonnas, bleeding hearts on display,
(at which my heart sank)
in the presence of that faintly foul
snuffed-out-candle odor, like a morgue for the soul,
we were following the recommended quick way.

Yet I couldn't help noticing how feet would slow;
it was almost on tiptoe
we arrived at the chalky-grey street's fresh air.
Our talk had been all about crossing over border,
Channel, realm, or time zone —
problems, problems in longed-for returns
from the years' incomprehensions . . .
and it seemed to accompany an English-style scone
the one thing we could order
was a pot of their *Thé des poètes solitaires.*

Disorientation

That newly fledged hedge sparrow
that flutters in the aura
of a neon lamp among the laurels
activates this height of summer
on pools with their reflected glories
where rain, nostalgic for the sky,
evaporates as heat
relentlessly returns, and we
are suddenly that bit poorer.
Obits come from another day.
Late light glows behind the leaves;
it backs off, turns away,
and I can do no more.

Like when, just out of hospital
and trying to feel well,
you sense the place as fragile;
you see how two wood pigeons
have gone and built their nest
in branches over the garden fence,
scaring away such smaller birds
as those aligned on the top of one vast
motorway junction sign
for Canterbury, Sevenoaks, Dover and the coast
— these things themselves like a picture of health,
being more at home than you can be
in your curiously lost self-interest,
and the light too going west.

Four

What Have You

for Adrian and Margaret

And even if it was the Greek word
you saw, what equally caught your eye
as we paused by a small tomb yard,
each stone with its proffered pot or cup,
was a flapping red-black butterfly
stuck perhaps on the open lip
of a silvered can of Asahi Dry . . .
Yes, that's what struck your eye.

From the World

'. . . unconditions himself
from those circumstances . . .'

1

Now, their mothballed power station
underneath a cloudy sky,
it doesn't have that much to say
for itself in a glitter-less autumn light —
its wharves abandoned, still and tidy
cranes, oil storage, not a trace
of smoke from three red-and-white-striped chimneys
overlooking pine-topped islands in the bay.

2

I'm staring out towards those islands
on a near horizon,
taking in their power station
as one who has mislaid the plot
or storyline, so it can tell
itself without me, as one who has forgot
and gone and left felt phrases
into which we disappear . . .
I'm staring out towards those islands.

3

Though wanting a story to carry us over
every twist and turn
in fates that wound you up here,
here I've wound up, nonetheless.
You see me in vacant or in pensive mood
and it's as if I'd lost it,

lost the thread of one
staring towards those pine-topped islands'
sights for sore eyes, or that eyesore
of a moth-balled power station.

4

But still glimpsed pine cones, tombs, wave-curved
declivities and yacht-hull shapes
add up to a drawn-out meaning
when carved birds peck at wooden grapes,
blue crows had cleared their throats this morning
and in a daze I might discover
how, pressures past, it points towards
possibilities in other words.

5

You see blue or white rags flap at poles;
they outline oyster farms and if not
tales themselves stand in for one —
which might as well be about that moth-balled power station
setting off the beauty of their beauty spot.

The Last Resort

For the ones who go and those about to stay,
two autumns: they're turning decay
in another of the spa towns money forgot
to contradictory signs and tokens —
like ripened apples or purple potatoes,
dropped leaves borne down-river, for ever
alighting to drift where the ducks sun themselves.
And I gaze at deserted bed- and bath-rooms
of bankrupted hotels . . .
Their proprietors had nothing else to do but walk away.

Where, once upon a time, there were stories to tell
now it's all maybe, maybe and perhaps
for ones bitten by mosquitoes
at a terraced vantage point
with smoke columns rising from rice-field fires,
the ones who must endure this season's
boredoms, its nervous collapse;
they're fretful about what, not leaving, they'll miss
and grieve for younger selves, ones
long-squandered on a promise,
and gaze at those hotels like scuttled battleships.

Nowhere in Particular

'Another morn than ours!'
Thomas Hood

Look, then, at places most times we don't see
being nowhere in particular,
not in another country . . .
Look at this taciturn spot on the planet
where tree shadow's striped over velvety moss
with verdigris, maple leaves, stones —
a place to be waiting for some person or persons.

Hold on, though, the thing is he was waiting for a death;
and in back of sleep I heard
a tearful phone call from the small hours
of a day to include her shroud,
this nowhere in particular, a quiet and tacit
turn of events through the night
when plans for our weekend would have to be abandoned.

Can't say, but about five the room filled with din.
It was the newsboy's
bike, the crows' chatter —
and havering over quite what would be wise
to do in our long run
of autumns for who it is goes and who stays
was not any better . . .
Dawn-light at curtains, the mourning could begin.

Frost Shadows

'Ich sage dir nicht oft genug,
daß ich dich liebe.'

Günter Eich

1

Treacherous in frost shadows
on the wrong side of a house,
or down hill curves
where the sun can't reach, here, love's
problems come tumbling out of a whiteness.
They leave us bruised and dazed as
even on warmer days like these
it seems that head among the lilies
in a framed photo just had to idealize
you, your wide myopic eyes
and married life like a cracked gutter
haemorrhaging water —
or rage which, clotted, couldn't be relieved.

2

So for a week you lived
still, silent in Intensive Care:
for us a week of airfare
bargains, bandages, nurses'
and doctors' crises,
night vigils, shouting fits,
regrets, and last visits
from children too young to know why
they were saying that goodbye.

3

Poor head, you would receive
attention, about to leave,

like never in life before —
as if all the people we couldn't love more
were summed up in this death.
Then your funeral wreath
and keening choir's
background noise just made it worse,
as did the high priest's prayer.

4

But when the casket was opened you were
lying unmoved with rimmed glasses on
and seemed the only one
amid our melting floods,
our fatal lack of appropriate words,
who hadn't had to suffer your funeral.
There, there, now I've said it all.

The Reproduction of Winter

Then with condensation streaming
on an early window pane
and, further, saturated sunlight
staining a white wall where tree shadow's
stencilled over it in tangles
starts a day of squall and bluster,
a day that just can't make its mind up
whether to be rain or shine.

Showers nobody had forecast
tipple from the cloud-drawn edge
to a shifting weather front.
Now towards us on a bridge
come scurrying, with no umbrellas,
caught-out spectres in the haze
and glitter of a river's vistas.

We're dazzled by furiously sunlit pavement.
Lately detached, the foliage
is pasted flat on asphalt.
Yes, that's where the old year went.
All over, now, the rain has eased.
An era's ending or there starts
some indifferent phase.

Behind the station, vacancies
gape between post-bombing homes;
and it's like your death or yours
had helped out with the clearance programmes;
it's like somebody else's wars
stripped from the few rheumatic trees
leaves and left them to define
the quick in terms of the deceased.
Their twigs scratch at a sky
where squall and blustery wind-gust
are lowering heads as if for the grace
at a skeletons' feast.

Drawing a Line

Raised house-fronts whose doors are windows,
choruses of seagulls on a sea-wall,
breezes, flares, fed ducks, passersby
with no deadlines, nothing at all
to do but follow
river curves towards far shores —
they make a day to improvise
on water reflections, sky's
evolving cloud-forms, and the shades
of night that flow
down through fishermen's houses,
boats hoved over yonder
across the way from home doors . . .
a day to stroll or wonder,
a day just to stand round inspecting the air.

That flying V of dusk-tinged geese,
migrants to another shore,
points off, moving on
in the clear of a wave-reflected sky,
as if the time had come and gone
for them to draw a line
under this failed self left alone
to curl up and die;
but circumstantial evidence
points off in every direction,
and though you may want to move on
like the day, to have some closure
watching its flashes of late light go hence,
though you may want to be drawing a line
with time, it can't be done.

On the Scene

Sun setting over that sea horizon
was a Spanish shriek mark, like a sign
for their tourist information,
or lower case first-person singular
painted on the scene.

Here was some local material loss.
You're sloping off, beside yourself
among those stands of pine;
and to hush your inner story,
grief's painted on the scene.

The scene is a very good listener
for things you'd never dream
of revealing to the likes of me,
intent on out-staring this loneliness
by gazing right into its face.

All in Our Day

Among the autumn's wreckage and election,
as an old bus coughs out gouts of black
on its switch-back road,
still mountain airs caress our faces;
hedge-hopping birds maintain their courses;
stray clouds sprawl across far peaks;
and us in our swarming littlenesses,
we're not to be cowed
by a cold wind here where even the rock speaks.

Rust-coloured lava and the green-toned lake
were being worshipped, as was promised,
by a queue of Sunday traffic
that snaked up our local dead volcano —
and not to be outdone
the season had been treating us
to typhoons, earthquakes, landslides, floods . . .
Remnants of that ruined autumn,
we're to live them, like somebody
here for the duration —
live them, yes, as if from settled choice.

Holding World

1

As news broke and press conferences occurred,
outside, storm-ruffled birds of prey
came wheeling across the wall-high panes.
Goodness, they looked scared.

Weakly fortressed from a world of harms,
that cawing by a few brave crows
was deceived too in the faint dawn's glint
on fingers of dwarf palms.

At this point in any particular year's
progress round the sun
their leaves press against each window glaze
a green embrace, and that's your lot.

Balcony shrubs, blooms, herbs in trays
withstand the first typhoon;
and though I'll think of them shivering with tears,
of course they're not, they're not.

2

That thought's just taken from the faces
of those reunited after years
survived in one of the Cold War's
most fearful lost causes.

They're brought back from oblivion,
handed flowers, fêted,
and the plague on both their houses
gets into our homes.

3

With signs of life around a corpse
at this season's lookout
on sea views at a hilltop's
temple, by its temple bell,
we glimpse boats in noon's dazzle.

Often now I'm out of breath
stopped on hillside paths with pines
and practically unclouded scenes,
scenes too reminiscent
of her, dead in her prime.

The lost had found a way back when
from our point of no return
these things seemed tainted, shut
in upon themselves, and gone,
as if death were a metaphor,
a metaphor for what?

4

Grown nearer in the latest breeze
leaves dither, glint as sun
breaks through another front and these
tremulous heights of branches
bend over backwards to where rice fields
with tender ranks of up-shoots
are empty but for a heron or gull.

Victims of national uses for strangers,
sad celebrities, they're carried
back to an unknown home world
and held by all this strangeness;
see, it reaches to embrace both them and us.

Mortuary Passport

1

After all the lamentations,
tears falling off our faces
for a wife, a mother, dead at forty-four,
she could not be laid to rest —
nobody mentioned any mortuary passport
needed to carry her onto the plane.
Illegally, they had exported her ashes,
were lucky not to have them confiscated
travelling with the family luggage
twelve or so hours to Milan from Narita
in the chill of a cargo hold.

2

After all, she had to be brought home.
There a local railway station's
portico in delicious shade
framed her seaport's northern suburb,
its ferries, tugs, container ships
black against an azure skyline;
there a few hot minutes' climb
brought us where she was laid to rest,
all paperwork completed,
her illegal sojourn over and done.

3

There, there, there she had come home,
a living face among those roses
on her tombstone in the wall
with photograph's ingenuous look
even as her young son struck it
right beneath a cypress tree
in the little cemetery
at Pegli, in Genoa,
overlooking her Ligurian sea.

4

Black glimmers of its restless motions
out beyond a harbour mole
lured us after night had fallen.
Her town's and promenade's lights turned on
and the docks' illumination
multiplied that fairyland.
A straggle of pilgrims strolled the shore,
our children's voices on the air,
us brought together by her death
then separated out down crane-lined streets
past lurid posters, lit haunts, bars
on a bus ride through the underworld
of that seaport's normal dark
and there, there, there she had come home.

5

Now then, given the above,
when a wind lifts and life's for the living,
let the jib fill, the boom swing
on a tack across this storied bay
and, despite love's seasickness
like grief at the stresses of yesterday,
drop off the old blue-hulled yacht's aft
into a Shelleyan swell
as the mountains make an end of it
at Portofino, in silhouette,
falling straight down to the sea.

The Empire of Light

for Giulia

When out of the subway we climbed, dusk's darkened
sky came to meet us
there in the form
of a mid-blue hue from the sun's after-light
screened by warmly off-white clouds;
they didn't seem to move at all
beyond a balconied grey house-end
with darkly pointing leaves,
its lamp lit above a lintel and door
over that embassy wall . . .

You noticed!
Said so in the street by a bankrupt hotel's
annex where I stayed
those dozen years before
when the least glimpse of that perimeter fence
with flag limp on its pole
would be sign enough to start up resentments, fears;
but here, as you're beside me
pointing at this blue,
I see now an embassy gloaming spells out
that even the impossible can happen too

— which is how it was with us, to say the least.

Five

Loud Weather

Home, home on this pulmonary night,
a hurricane-force wind
hoots round the chimney at three in a morning
of squally blast and blight
and, yes, there's a smell of some kind
like flood water traces in brickwork and plaster.

It's a smell that lingers, meaning
for you this far north the life's to be known
in an insomnia's Cimmerian dark
or at least with that low, oblique bluster
of a perpetual twilight.

Airily thin across Baltic archipelagoes
yet one more diffused dawn
fires out clouds above their hill-lines.
Here, on a trip through the vast inhospitable,
nature in its element would find
limits to what can be set right.

It's a smell that lingers, meaning
where there's no end of trouble I need
all of you with me, you old so-and-sos.
I need you in all honesty.
It's as if I could still feel the cut cord bleed.

Ratifying Kyoto

In a transitory light, you see
low sun's throwing elongated shadows
of branches, wires, telephone poles;
it's casting them across snow remnants
or a house wall's second storey
where your own, entangled with them,
(as if you were that shadow cast)
tells of only chill deferrals —
no end of them at a winter's end.

It's one of those underprivileged moments
when the protocols of snow
are pushed aside to exhaust neglect,
when, talk notwithstanding, some holes
are poked in the sky, in the sky
and in our arguments.

So you ratify Kyoto
criss-crossing the city in search of traces
where each grief and trauma
came to be expressed: you're here
to find a future habitat, a home, or
roof above our heads at least; the space is
still sadder, no wiser and you,
you haven't a pallid idea.

Public Holiday

Flopped down, pigeons sun themselves
where two rivers merge and flow
as one out to the Inland Sea.
It's a place for picnics, trysts,
where, in shallows, paddling infants
trawl with nets, where egrets nest;
in step-down falls they're dead still, yes,
but not dead, seen by alien lovers
teasing each other on the green riverside.

Yes, and it strikes a contemporary
this fluvial coming together
draws on the public holiday air
worn by a clear sky, stirring trees,
the stepping stones a traffic jam
of mid-stream children and their parents.

When stiffened breeze vexes reed edges,
it's about all we can hope for —
real traffic stopped up on bridges;
but the river flows still as ever
past pain, and past attentions
stirred in the sudden appearance of clues
known from all those years before.

It's like stepping in the same river twice:
whether they're dead, or only gone,
she's here again, and she is too,
her greying fringe blown forward,
the other that thin you feared she'd vanish
if so much as turning sideways —
which is what both went and did,
companions of that moment, ones
who took the edge off solitude.

And I was forgetting myself but for this
as if what joy is were mislaid
but for these ordinary reminders
in vague guitars, cries, barbecues . . .
For this, I listen to their native strains,
being apart, a part of elsewhere
rubbed in on a daily basis
when police cordon off these shallows,
trawl them too, you can't say why.
Yet here you are, undeniably here,
with a flower-shop quay's blooms on display
where two rivers merge and flow
out to the Inland Sea.

Glaswegiana

for Adam Piette

'. . . vienen de la taberna voces,
Y luego un tren que pasa
Agita largos ecos como bronce iracundo.
No es el juicio aún . . .'

Luis Cernuda

1

Provided the moon above their airport is full,
a flagstaff has its stray staffage
of students relaxing on a fine spring day,
the city's still visited by seagulls,
picture restorers are joking at their task
and pink blossom streams from a wind-twitched tree,
the sun has dispelled a Calvinist sky
and a street's blues musician really can play
where are theatres, clouds and shadows,
a river walk's not defaced that much,
clearly the stone can remember its blackness,
ancestors neither forgotten or ashamed,
Clydebank's currents promise kyles and islands . . .
and if these are at least provided,
not merely offered as a lure and check,
then, yes, you might just be able to decide.

2

Come here at least to sniff the air
in an Ingram Street tearoom or across George Square,
I'm led past photos of local street weapons
to William Scotts, Eardleys, Paolozzi's toys,
past office staff on renovated porches
sunning themselves for some lunchtime ease,

or art students feeling how lucky they are
even if fated for call-centre studies —
so what, so what on a day like today
when sunlight obliges our shadows
to be last pieces of an interlocking puzzle
here as I sniff the air.

3

Familiar strangeness in a half-timbered gable
caught as your red car's breasting a rise
and the season's weather, changeable,
cloud shadow skiffing a rampart's remnants
leads to some fable-like Sunday lunch features
where later the actors all loll at their places
and a months-old baby's asleep in the sun,
I imagine how it might be to live
here in this straggle of enclaves and closes
even as my hosts are preparing to leave . . .

4

Then beyond the high-arched windows
in a panelled conference room,
Glasgow recedes through layering haze,
its walled canals, a smoke of gulls,
tenements, wharves, and shipyard cranes.
Out beyond Victorian casements
as fate works its erasures
already I can sense an *esprit d'escalier*
rising now vistas of the not-to-be
thin and waver and slip away.

5

Still later, at an attic dormer window,
this drunk man looks out over fields
as dawn light's starting to show
a version of home through its back-garden fences,
council-flat brick, and wild pasture.
Like a secret love story, or suddenly revealed
aversion to home, he'll be gone tomorrow,
still can't stay; but, all the same,
there's a karaoke voice now as good as hums to him:
will ye nae come haeme, my Rabbie,
will ye nae come haeme?

Huis Clos

'¿Es el infierno así?'
        Luis Cernuda

But at the candidate's dinner, my heart
was somehow not in it —
much to be said on the tip of the tongue,
many words uttered best bitten back
in that crepuscular restaurant
there with the other ones: 'What! *you* here too?' —
those lording it over the servile, the lost
resentfully chewing, and you . . .

yet another reason to be up and gone;
but there was no leaving, the service
slow with our orders, wine glasses, desserts . . .
interminable waits between courses!
Still, I could taste that melancholy strain
in wallpaper music's far-off things
and, doubtless too, a distant train
shedding its echoes like some brass trumpet —

though not for the judgment day, not yet.
So if I struck the board and cried
into those shadows, '*Bon nuit, mon ami!*'
that isn't to say he was talking to me
as we ate, drank, were merry
for tomorrow some would be wasting their time.
No, no, this was not the last judgment;
this was the trial by false bonhomie.

Evacuation Drill

'a future only beckons beyond airspace.'
David Pascoe

When the alarm went off at Glasgow Airport,
we each trooped out to a holding area
under the noses of an Airbus or two.

Although that sky looked clear enough
for landing and take-off, as to the future
(another story altogether),
it beckoned beyond those near hill contours,
lochs, firths, braes, and the purple heather.

Topiary, lawn, red brick and sandstone,
the lengthened shadows as we banked above
were becoming by extension
all I might have lost through this —
like a faraway story of unrequited love;
from the cumulo-nimbus, one ae fond kiss . . .

and then its wings were engulfed in cloud cover.
Down on the tarmac before at Glasgow
there had been no kind of bomb-scare,
terrorist attack, or technical failure.
At cruising height first drinks would flow
until the entire trip started to appear
like a routine exercise, a training alarm
for the management of that hope, that fear;
for one ae fond kiss, and then whatever.

The Deficit

For one more rainy season with barely any rain,
as if June's humid heat could burn
off recidivist self-concern
to leave this side street in a bit of town
where the water tank outside our window is grey,
its commentaries of aerials
stack against sky like they mean to say
something or other with their strokes and tails.
Asphalt-men shovel at heaps of black
tipped from a dump-truck's back;
the fumes float far as roofs
past balconies jam-packed with things —
umbrellas, laundry, house plants
in a makeshift arrangement that brings
random sensations like almost being home . . .
which gets us back to the murmur and hum
of traffic along an expressway
across these eastern mountains.
Baffled by a screen of trees
waving like globalization protesters,
they get through nonetheless
with flashes, crash-bangs as of bedroom doors,
hailstones, and this world-size puzzle's
making up the deficit
in me, in us, or in anything else that won't fit.

So There

So there, those gawping gormless features,
a gargoyle's, finger between fat lips,
I used to gaze up at them, years back,
stumbling home in a pre-dawn haze
or at that third-floor window with her
talking in the small hours, look,
my momentary student self's so there
listening to her replies . . .
that now the monumental mason's
self-parodic caricature
battens on these rare occasions
as if they too informed against me,
as if I'd plainly missed the future
and didn't realize.

A London Afterlife

'for he could but gape at his other
self in this other anguish . . .'
                    Henry James

Glimpsing pellucid summer sky
past cliff-face brick and glass façade,
alright, suppose you did come back
for a single night and found
floral tributes, draped flags, slogans,
wanted posters for the missing
identified, since, among those dead;
let's suppose you did come back,
and met him at a bar somewhere
near the crime scene, look, its blood stains
marking still one fair stone wall,
late, late what with the trains . . .

                    *

He had already got in a beer.
Remotely, sirens sounded.
A slender breeze was soughing.
From all points of the compass,
distraction's old sick hurry
of roads being taken and not taken
came barrelling into or out of that square.

The square itself lay motionless
inside its railings' thick detail.
At the bar, came huffing and puffing
about moth, rust, you don't say . . .
For London that's nothing unusual;
the city absorbs it all,
indifferently lifts words away.

                    *

The square itself lay motionless.
A child lay asleep in its pram
by rose garden, statues, memorial benches,
leaves a dark canopy suspended in air.
But you weren't so easy to talk to, like
family he'd not seen for many a year
with issues, resentments, reserve . . .
So how few wanted us to come to any harm?

He'd got the job we both went in for,
had already had an eventful career,
was a little burned-out, sure, overstretched
moonlighting for the papers, yes;
yet his every anecdote's divided aim
gaining neither love nor praise,
no, he hadn't changed that much;
we still looked the same.

                    *

I liked him; but he didn't recognize me,
an alter ego or what-have-you
pausing to shake hands at a corner,
and hurried on his way
to glimpse from one of the wandering buses
another poster, for a stray cat,
stuck up on that lamp post there where —
pellucid blue above the serried,
cliff-face brick and glass façade —
London's slotted sky would squander
wisps of cloud across void spaces
as mementos, mementos for those lost lives.

July 2005

Not Lost

In haste: from a late lunch to *The Last Supper*
there were fingers raised expressing
belief or disbelief at just such a proper
confusion of people and things,
at such triangulated spaces in between them . . .

Like when we were hurrying from one square to another,
when somewhere between Michelangelo
and via Giasone del Maino, her mother
let fall she was lost, completely lost,
and our younger one said 'Well, I'm not lost
because I don't know where I'm going' —
disarming those street-grids as never before
with her spirit and the letter.

Occasion to Revise

There on a strip of neglected land
in an unknown or little known
corner of Verona's
inner suburbs behind the fair,
a strip providing neighbourhood owners
with paths, a patch of earth to foul,
I watched my step as words, words, words
came back to mind
and a tang of cat piss in the air
was catching at my throat.

'Beware of what you want when young;
you'll get it in middle age . . .'
were the words came back to mind
while sullen heat that afternoon
made shade provided by
a condominium's height
so much more my place to be.
A poor maltreated sheep-dog bitch,
rescued, cared for, given a home,
strained to do her business
on some yellow grass.

That tang of cat piss in the air
catching at my throat
had been a territorial, an era-ending scent
but for the nothing ever over,
no end of story, fault, palaver
and need to have a care.

The House Guest

'"So you think you're changed, do you?"
"I'm afraid I am, Sir," said Alice.'

Lewis Carroll

He was walking right out of the sun
with long bow and arrows;
and, as shadows crossed behind us,
discarded time returned
in the face of someone
I'd not seen for years on end.

He was taking us to see
another Buddha, with head turned
in its golden frame —
one looking back as if concerned
for his followers, such
stragglers as us,
shoeless on the wooden walkways.

He was sleeping below a pagoda
high up on the mountain;
and gripping the rail from my fear of heights,
I was wiping Chinese
desert sand from strained eyes
that watered in the sun.

He was asking me what he had done
to be so unforgiven,
telling me he too had changed,
though you'd know him anywhere —
anywhere like that pagoda,
serried, untempting rooftops below
and hazed green hills between —
and not that the past had been set to rights,
but its time had gone.

Après le Déluge

A rainstorm finds the upstairs open;
and its fierce downpour streams
over a ledge heaped up with papers
through mosquito screens.

Now my faded blue ink smudges
are half rubbed out by rain
in our own White Rabbit's house
where late, I'm late again.

So much of it's already gone
the remainder disappears,
deleting us from hoarded papers
in an Alice's pool of tears.

Kyoto Protocols

'And this same progeny of evils comes
From our debate, from our dissension:
We are their parents and original.'
                    William Shakespeare

Past a pond by the hall where the protocols were formed,
a squadron of pigeons over-flew the rowboats;
water lights flickered on bark hereabouts.

Meanwhile, perpetual helicopter blades
stuttered and a heron held its pose,
its silhouette through stakes of a sorry pavilion.

This beautification enforcement area
had council retainers spiking last remains
of picnic sites and barbecues . . .

Then the more they set up the fried food stalls,
the more plum and cherry leafage falls
and keeps on falling with a look of goodbye.

                    ★

A stone's throw from the Imperial Palace
red leaves with rain holes hung on in the blue,
sunlight behind them tracing out their veins;
and then across our temple district,
there were policemen posted on each corner
as if to protect a protest-silenced zone
for one with the fate of the planet on his conscience,
and that tired face to save.

                    ★

Below four bridges, the mallards, cranes, blue crows
would seem about to rise

even as buses with wired blank windows
are parked at either end of them
to stake out reed beds and the stepping stones.

This confluence of two streams gives
just so many crisscross lines —
the river-walks, cables, waterfalls, perspectives
dividing towards and away as glides
of inland seagulls also take us by surprise.

                    *

Sparrows flitted from the clear to the obscure
through autumn days we'd spent
in a sea of yellow gingko leaves
trying to amend lives before it's too late,
too late, already, to be sure.

Last tints in the fading atmosphere
had formed a tainted aftermath
where whatever we'd wanted when young
remained unremembered so long
it's gone with ants and mosquitoes of those times.

                    *

That speckled grey pigeon on a telephone wire
trained a beady, rust-coloured eye
on us all in the same boat as a family;
and like one who speaks out of turn, inanely smiles,
you were rowing it slowly back in to shore
while, elsewhere, the hand that didn't sign the paper
waved through leaves at the Golden Pavilion
catching a glimpse of this city through its heat-haze,
unusually warm in those mid-November days,
autumnal decay and fall deepening.

Auspicious Motives

1

Halfway down the women's slope,
you catch an undecided sky
beyond late autumn remnants
on standoffish trees.

Above the National Museum's
reminiscent spikes and brick,
gleam snow-coated mountains
candied in a setting sun.

No trouble smudged across them
though some there might have been,
afforested slopes in their allure
near through dusk-toned air.

You see, our day, it has its moments;
what fears there might have been
are in an instant borne away
letting me alone at least.

Fast trouble, no longer missed,
leaves us to it in sun setting
above constructed skylines
and trees almost bare.

2

This afternoon, eternal nowhere,
houses neither new nor falling,
bears up with a cloud-grey air,
some bicycles, some passersby
and not a sign of dusk tone.

Girls' voices ring like birdsong
from a hidden garden's pine.

It's all brought on by tiredness, sky,
or else by being at a loose end
of time, though there are none.

This afternoon, each day's unique
atmospheric effects have come
where life's effaced from chances
of anything like resemblances
between this and another one.

3

But on the bridge, late evening,
its lanterns orange in a night
of cloudless climes and starry neon,
dark gulfs between each point of light,
it's like the question won't arise
given that interstellar vacuum
and the curved sky's
endlessly attractive silence.

Thanks to our gravity, our airiness,
not too chilly, too, this evening,
I'm here still by the parapet —
which is something, being here,
minute in earth's shadow, yet
head up, heading home.

4

Home, like that house by the corner,
would be a bonsai nursery.
Sculpted pines, geraniums,
walnut bushes, sword-blade palms
spill across pavement round its door;
and there we'll see lamps burning late,
letting slip signs of an intimate

survival, life forms all the more
difficult to fathom, too far away
from such passing alien fauna . . .
Strange home, that house by the corner,
is itself compacted in decay.

5

Rain's morse, this fingered tom-tom,
on a bat's wing black umbrella
was beating out its timely message
while I headed back towards home.
Viper thoughts, red trunks of pine,
were writhing round a lotus pond.

The rain was lucid, cooling, free
of any envy, rage, resentment —
whether mine, or others' of me;
it let a calmer atmosphere
settle to some needful errand,
a message, the sky had sent me.

6

At the white bridal house, more sky
opened out in sequenced currents,
cloud groups, swirls of energy
convergent on that point.

More traffic at a five-way junction
flowed round where the river bridge
curved towards birds on a wire
airing their pitch-contours.

And here death stopped for me
(a gold-black temple-roofed hearse)

as the *walk—don't walk* light changed,
me picking up my pace.

With snow-dusted, sacred mountain
blocked in behind, I'm back again,
my awkward bow for the still chauffeur
after all those years.

7

Old lady with your straight white hair
and sucked-in mouth, you hesitated
at that zebra crossing, were
meaning, a figure and ground,
in this niche for new buds swelling,
where cloud-covered water
flowed below three bridges —

as if by helping you cross over
I'd merge into community;
but don't, don't ever arrive,
am left to be defined
against fresh sun, fast cloud
seen from a room overlooking balconies
with fast tints on their lines;

and goaded beyond all endurance
about what I can or can't sing,
will turn on whoever, fly in defence
of colleagues, mother tongues,
find myself outside a 7-Eleven
under a clear sky, trying to govern
my own and be forgiven.

Cul-de-sac

Slid screens open on the failing day
in a mish-mash of roofs,
furze cooling up a hill slope
seen from their interior
with conversation pieces
and frayed bits of conversation . . .

One talking point will be the storm
promised by a breeze
among bamboo leaves beyond the pale
of bamboo poles and wire fences.
Meanwhile, monkeys, wild boar, deer
trespass through an early dusk —

skidaddle as the wind gusts blow
grass blades in perpetual waves
of deepening greens
watched behind slid screens
by mismatched lives
with their nowhere else to go.

The Dolls' House

No, we've no need of a nightingale floor,
our enemies are far away
or not at all . . .
Even so, staircases creak;
I tread them in a depth of night
on tiptoe —
because not wanting to wake
this whole fun house, a haunted one,
or tunnel of love in the darkness.
Here cupboard doors swing open;
light-switch strings
are dangling down to tickle my face:
I can't but feel not quite,
or only just at home in our own home.

Today the house is like a circus.
Half-tamed clowns, mad animals,
artistes in leotards
are tumbling over each other,
bumping into the too much furniture.
With screams, howls, rage,
hand-coloured streamers in the air
to surprise a grandmother,
we're each of us trying to act our age,
to have a good scold or cry . . .
but when all's said,
all done, well, then we'll put the dolls to bed.

Old Loves

Next morning, not long after daybreak,
the neighbour woman across our street,
right elbow on a worn chair arm,
lifting thick curtains with her left hand,

leaned from the window of a ground-floor flat;
and there she was, Hendricke Stoffels,
out of the Edinburgh *Young Woman in Bed*,
who appeared to be looking around for her cat;

but what with the warm, unusually warm
sun touching her, and with that companionate
momentary glimpse, a trick of eye or light,
it was Rembrandt van Rijn himself shaking us awake.

Six

The Spelk

Like when a window pane just after sunset
flares and lets this spelk
(yes, that's the word) or rotten wood splinter
stick in the skin of my palm,
I'm back on a bike that's slipped through a crack
in the terrace and shot down the brew
to ramshackle sheds, hen-coops, house-ends
where streets break apart into dirt.

My mother would coax them out with a needle,
lift skin along the life line
as if to tell where we're originally from
etymologically speaking —
eras and epochs of kids' minor hurt
lit up by that word
like when a window pane just after sunset
flares and, without a thought, thoughts revert.

On the Mobile

Beyond the Lifestyle Protection Centre
there were choices to be made
and ragged, grey plastic bags
snagged on the branches of pollarded trees
being dug out around their roots
no doubt for transplanting to who-knows-where.

'I've got to give him time to fall in love with me,'
said the girl with a mobile at her ear
as she boarded our train for Crewe
and I was just about to say . . .

But then we shuddered off from the platform.
Threads of bungalows would fray
in landscapes with seagulls on filter-beds,
ones where my first wife's uncle
commuted to his job with British Rail.

Past willow-herb embankments,
equivocal points and sidings,
it was like she'd given me a moment's pause
to tie up the loose ends of time.

So then those summers seemed all one
missed connection, the betrayal
of more than enough to recall
how little I know about love . . .

Yet right when you're wondering whatever could happen
in these slight returns of life,
it happens, it suddenly happens
I'm back on my night watchman's nightshift
reading *Hard Times* by the light
of a drinks dispensing machine;
I'm back to some Luna Park, or Disneyland forlorn,

seeing coach windows fill up with her voice
as she gives him time to fall in love
and we pass flaked bridges, pubs, and villas . . .
It's almost like being reborn.

Unheimlich Leben

Seeing that far-fetched look of yours,
again I have you coming home
from Valparaíso, as it might be,
to the Isle of Ely.

Maltings, greens, a sunken lane
seen then on a daily basis
turn aside, as if withdrawn,
at your coming home —
home to hear how the natives complain
and with so little reason,
to find its quiet brick streets and walks
grating on you all the more.

I see them as though through your eyes,
those drowned lands with their roundabouts,
industrial parks, estates
now high and dry
when a local bus fails to materialize . . .
But what would these glimpses be for
if not to make peace with our places and times?
Leafage is thick like the summers before,
your guess, as good as mine.

Like a Reminder

With sycamore leaves backing into the breeze
like strollers on a prom, exposed
to record-breaking heat who've gone
at dusk to cool their heads,
we found ourselves by crowded exits,
bus stops, taxi ranks . . . and seized
on tabloid headlines, hectic, flushed
from weeks of cloudless sun.

The various leaves looked frazzled, stressed,
as grass does in a hose-pipe ban;
I saw them wilt, or barely stir
when that breeze broke down;
like trains across the network, one
failing made another late —
so late it's cancelled and, non-plussed,
we wait like statues there.

While sun behind the staggering trees
of a summer thickness rimmed
raggle-taggle fringes round their tops
with halos of slant rays,
from plate-glass waiting rooms, still, come
soundscapes, murmured plans or hopes for
that same night in terms of each
half-fathomable phrase.

Then English spoken on the platform
by way of blank apologies
at our latest home-made chaos
stretched a point where last light
indicates the sycamore leaves,
and though time seemed a series of
cost-benefit sums, in this home from home
it's off-set by those trees.

And a Name

'Is this called "Mercyside"?'
             Bob Dylan, May 1965

The flash of seagulls' wings in sunlight,
white across some heaped grey cloud,
makes eyes follow them in flight
above a warehouse, long bricked-up,
with FIREPROOF DEPOSITORY in tiled lettering.

I watch them tumbling through this airspace
over businesses gone under
like that fish-and-chip restaurant,
a shadow of its household name
formed in dust where the lettering's torn off.

Here August weeds are at their proudest;
great stalks sprung through its forecourt flags
announce the end of another local era;
and, at stoplights, as engine noise dies down,
just listen to the seagulls cry.

Heart & Company

'plus vite . . . que le cœur d'un mortel'
Charles Baudelaire

Once more, fearful of missing the train,
dad taxis me to Lime Street station
and, think of that, we're lost again
before each temporary roundabout
or work in progress, each crash barrier,
sculpture, traffic light, deviation;
we're flummoxed by all this renovation
for the European City of Culture Year.

Out on the town, then, with a son
and family, dad's got lost again
after one more unfamiliar
turn, caught in the wrong filter lane.

So there we are among improvements
down a brand-new, dead-end street
far as bollards, flowerbeds,
a game of penalties going on . . .

But now they've fixed my mother's heart.
Its leaky valve's replaced, the veins
a street map of some building site;
and there we stop to ask directions
of a crone, perhaps, all aches and pains
who keeps the till in a charity shop
and, peering, pokes a finger right
out beyond the back end of nowhere.

2006

Enigmas of August

Grasshoppers, prone, alerted by our wheels,
they leap up at the windshield,
are bounced towards parched verges —
those caught between our wiper-blades
being swept aside like chaff, like corpses
in some Bible plague.

You recall the outnumbering dead;
now we, the living, outnumber them all,
are greeding them into the ground
under our subsidized lifestyles and crops,
those bladed off to each edge of the road
from that moving asphalt.

Life on the road! Look, moving asphalt
rises to meet us, commits its forces;
and we're like those who'd blame a loved one
dead in a terror or air-strike attack
for going and dying and leaving us
lonely, leaving us too much alone . . .

This same afternoon, ants beneath my feet,
hither and thither on laid patio,
are frantically searching a flagstone;
a scrawny tomcat, shooed away,
freezes and stares hard before sloping off,
that mortally offended.

Likewise, as one who'd despise her
abandoning me to myself, again,
as one supposed to be at home
here with the distance and cities of the plain,
I'm likely to murmur a 'Thank you',
she then replying, 'You're welcome';
and nobody any the wiser.

Lying Figures

'Creature biforcate e logo-immuni
mi sorsero davanti,
invulnerabili alla verità.'
Valerio Magrelli

'Baue, wenn die Stundenuhr rieselt,
Aber weine nicht die Minuten fort
Mit dem Staub zusammen,
Der das Licht verdeckt.'
Nelly Sachs

1

Nervous janglings in the leaves
against a mid-blue evening sky,
the columns of black poplars form
screens to block off distances.

Now an orange full moon surges
up above them, in the clear;
we're gazing at it round the edges
of a bathroom window pane.

The poplar branches pitch and sway;
it's like our middle ground had vanished,
like those things were all too close
and too far away.

2

Balcony guardrails' vertical rectangles,
scaffolding walkways on latest apartments
wall us in a lost past.

A grille intersected by poplar tree tangles,
black apertures, the not-yet-bedrooms,
they wall us into a future too.

3

Well then, to get back self-possession
they're viewed at an angle of ninety-degrees
by one woken after an afternoon nap;

and steadily to outface recession,
textures, tastes, words, fore- and hindsight,
I touch ground in a perpetual present
of what had to be, and what hadn't.

4

But there is a pain in the room
as I head for the toilet past midnight,
am groping about in an absence
of object relations, spaces between them,
sleeping loved ones not to disturb
like so much mental furniture . . .
But then if I turn on a night-light
that pain's gone into the dark.

5

Flaked paintwork, cracked plaster,
the scuff marks of slack time,
or ifs and buts you muster
start thoughts, shift them like furniture . . .

Yet in this invalid's living room
it's as if all perspectives but one
have been lost sight of with his future,
every other aspect gone.

6

And at a dead point in our summer
fighter-bombers loose their payloads,

de-house neighbour populations,
blood-spatter concrete, pock-mark roads . . .

Pre-emptive air strikes, as we speak,
make mockeries of UN truce terms.

At a dead point in our summer
the planes make work for building firms.

7

Referred pain starts as a malaise
in numbed limbs, trapped nerves, livid scars.
Recovery's days follow days
of referred pain like the malaise
from each spokesperson's crafted phrase
claiming perspective, justifying wars.
Referred pain starts in our malaise
as numbed limbs, trapped nerves, livid scars.

8

Then in that invalid's room once more
columns of figures, lying figures
form sums that make no sense for sure.
The numbers are expressions of
strained family ties, or lacking love,
and we're to take the blame for long
division, forever in the wrong,
must pay again what we had paid before.

9

Three magpies patrol this stalled site
in black and white uniform;
storm clouds behind, they alight
on its crane's still arm.

Some experimental birdsong
might be a blue-winged jay;
it's turning the lot articulate
as a thing to say.

10

Comes a hammering through flaked walls
and, equally, a smell of solvent
infiltrates dark, lowered shutters.
They're bolting scaffolding all around us.
We hear them josh in maybe Polish,
hear them plaster and paint façades.

At dusk, you let a fresh breeze come
to flush out our imprisoned air.
They're here again soon after dawn
bolting scaffolding all around us;
fellow lifers, they aim to communicate,
and their hammering keeps us company.

11

That grille's traversed by drizzling rain
now, as August is brought low
and a late cease-fire's still holding.
Disposal experts set to work
disarming red-ringed cluster bombs.

Layered cement dust you can't miss,
nor glass shards, nor stray billowing smoke.
Black apertures, room spaces look
like others' lost pasts, and futures too,
emptied of their folk by cluster bombs.

12

Then though there come divided figures,
talk-immune, blocked off from what's true,
to tread on your dreams of shared words,
am I less entitled to practise an art
of the possible with this building work
in brick-shaped tiles on a balcony floor
or bricks themselves of unfinished façades
for as long as we can take these things to heart?

Sound Advice

1

Like a Chinese paper orchestra
with cardboard box percussion section
now cicadas, monks' prayer sticks,
and hammers of house carpenters
come knock-knocking through a heat haze.

Meanwhile, round us, there are whirs
and ticks from the conditioners;
then come cries of van loud speakers
bringing boomed timbres, tinkling cymbals'
tacit wave-forms through still air.

Stunned from the drumming of an inner ear,
I'm advised by rustled news sheets,
martial anthems, sounding brasses
come on through this heat haze . . .
These too strike the note of home.

2

Like washboards or maracas,
those chorusing cicadas
drown out even our CD player
and yet you see no source for them,
invisible creatures of the heat;
from quivering leaves, their noise
dies down as dusk encroaches.

Then you hear night change its tune
to the whisper of far crickets
or cracks from an electric storm.
When heat returns, the racket's

back as applause at a party rally
swelling with every implausible thing
platform speakers say.

3

But listen, down this riverside
after dark you'll hear
mingle with the leaves and hisses
strains of practising musicians'
flutes, guitars, drums, saxophones . . .
The season's terror-struck madnesses,
anxieties at being here
dissolve a moment with these traces
of flattened and diminished tones,
and all their western intervals
invite us to be gone back home.

Exit Strategies

Life in an oblique light, autumn's
or daybreak's, comes
like drawn curtains out from flat cloud banks;
open, closed, whatever, it comes
down leaf-coloured hillsides'
casual jigsaws of roof-shapes and corners,
epochs in their building lines;
with intricate grammar, the light
attends to each detail, praises
existence, picks out leaves
still hinting at what made me stay.

There again, they look
like one more invitation
to be off and gone . . .

Such a rain-reflected stillness
falls from the weather front's edge this morning
as peculiar yellow tints
slip across paths of stuck-down leaves,
interleave far other times
with their maculate array,
that, because it's among last times
I will do this, items
from the city's reiterated years
are as likely telling me
what it is we could take from those years,
or must give away.

Drawing a Blank

Trust it to go and come down all day,
like blossom had arrived too soon
or paper weights were shaken, arms
flailing at one further flurry
of spread-sheets, minutes, *memento mori* . . .

We're all snowed under believe you me
with attachments, odds and ends,
plaster dust from an earthquake crack;
now the print-outs pile back
to try you, your spouse's, the children's
understanding, and some friends.

It happens you're asked to start again
and stumble on a crisis, fall
headlong clutching at last straws,
the world outside turned to a slurry
of white out on their fields.

*

Then look here at the snowed-in landscape's
buried house-fronts, burdened roofs,
or loneliness of long distances
melting up as clouds of mist
till the whole more or less disappears
beyond thaw-glistened roads.

Translated, anybody, see traffic lights
turn greener and the stray cars leave
across whiteboards with rubbed-out words
like one doomed for a term to talk
upon those widest-spread confusions
far distances also relieve.

With Eyes Closed

1

Maybe it's only the weather this evening,
those doodles of feathery cloud
like a scrawl spray-gunned across the blue,
but, instantly, I can imagine
cherry-tree avenues with not a soul on them,
leaf shade not shading anyone, mum,
and no, not a pale view of hills,
deep blue ones under that fainter sky
warm-tinged at its fringes.

2

You know why I've lined up so many excuses
yet can't help wanting to be out of here,
out of this too sticky air . . .
But dusk-lit, instantly, I can imagine
gaps between things are no more
than measurable spaces
and a lake's pink-reflected under that sky,
a river runs where it ought to be
and the far hills have taken up their places.

Notes

The Red Dusk: 'Anfield' is the football ground where Liverpool F.C. play when they are at home. Their shirts are red. In July 1919 Winston Churchill ordered a battleship and two destroyers to lie in the Mersey estuary as a precaution during the Policemen's Strike.

As Like as Not: The epigraph is from line 16 of John Donne's 'Hymn to God my God, in my Sickness'. The 'Zelkova' tree is a member of the elm family (Ulmaceae Zelkova serrata).

Raubkunst: The title means 'Stolen art' and is used to indicate those works confiscated from Jewish collectors during the Nazi period, which found their way into public or semi-public collections. There are on-going legal battles about the ownership of these works.

Totes Meer: ['Dead Sea'] is the name of a picture depicting wrecked German planes from the Battle of Britain period painted by Paul Nash and hanging in the Tate Gallery, London.

The Better Halves: The epigraph is from *The Chameleon Poet: A Life of George Barker (2001)*. The poet was a foreign teacher at Tohoku University for a few months during 1940. The Italian soccer team had their training camp in Sendai during the 2002 World Cup.

Stranded: The station is at Monterosso, the most northerly of the Cinque Terre on the Ligurian coast above La Spezia, Italy.

Silence Revisited: The poem is set at the mountain temple of Yamadera, Yamagata prefecture, where Bashō wrote the haiku included in *The Narrow Road to the Deep North* that is translated as the epigraph. The poem alludes to my 'Deep North' from *Lost and Found* (1997), inspired by a visit to the same place ten years before.

Mentioned in Dispatches: I cite most of the last line to F. T. Prince's 'Soldiers Bathing' first collected in his 1954 book of that name. I have no evidence beyond my father's memory of sixty years before that he was among the Intelligence Corps soldiers under Prince's command in Italy who may have helped to inspire that poem.

Hope Hospital: The penultimate line includes an allusion to 'Where then shall Hope and Fear their Objects find?' from Dr Johnson's poem 'The Vanity of Human Wishes' (1749).

Life is Good: The title alludes to a piece of conceptual art by Martin Vincent that consists of a brass plaque on wood with the inscription 'Life is Good in Manchester'. I'm grateful to David Mather for sending the postcard from the Manchester City Art Gallery.

Calm Autumn: The epigraph is the first of two unpublished verses of mine, written just before the Gulf War in 1991.

My Italy: The epigraph is from the last line of Petrarch's 'Italia mia' (no. 128 in the *Canzioniere*), a poem perhaps prompted by the war around Parma in the winter of 1344-45.

The Quick Way: 'Solitary poets' tea' is a blend of China and Darjeeling available at Mariage Frères, 30-32 rue du Bourg-Tibourg in the Marais, Paris.

From the World: The epigraph is from a review of Robert Browning's poetry by E. P. Hood, cited on p. 175 of Adrian Poole's *Shakespeare and the Victorians* (2004).

The Last Resort: The poem was prompted by and begins with Yosa Buson's haiku which I read in French: 'Pour celui qui part / pour celui qui reste — / deux automnes'.

Nowhere in Particular: The epigraph is the last line to Thomas Hood's 'The Death-Bed'. 'Nowhere in Particular', 'Frost Shadows', the third part of 'Holding World', and 'Mortuary Passport' are in memory of Lisetta Yoshimochi (1960-2003).

Frost Shadows: The epigraph is the last two lines of Günter Eich's 'Westwind' from *Botschaften des Regens* (1955). It reads: 'I did not say to you enough, / it's you I love.'

Drawing a Line: David Kelly (1944-2003) was the government scientist interviewed by a parliamentary committee over the 'dodgy dossier' of intelligence used to justify the invasion of Iraq. He committed suicide on 17 July 2003 in the aftermath of that experience which he described as 'worse than my PhD interview'. The poem is to his memory.

Holding World: This poem was occasioned by the repatriation of a few of the Japanese abductees kidnapped and taken to North Korea approximately thirty years before.

The Empire of Light: The title translates the French name for a painting by René Magritte, one also being vaguely recalled in 'Italian Poplars'.

Glaswegiana: The epigraph is from Luis Cernuda's 'Cementerio en la ciudad' [Cemetery in the city]: '. . . voices come from the tavern, / And then a train going by / Stirs long echoes like furious bronze. / It's not the judgment yet . . .' Cernuda taught Spanish at the University of Glasgow between 1941 and 1943.

Huis Clos: The title is from Jean Paul Sartre's 1944 play of the same name, usually translated as 'No Exit', a work containing the phrase 'l'enfer, c'est les autres' [hell is other people]. The epigraph is also from Cernuda's 'Cementerio en la ciudad' and reads 'Hell is like this?'

Evacuation Drill: The epigraph is the last sentence in David Pascoe's *Airspaces* (2004).

A London Afterlife: The epigraph is from Henry James's story 'The Jolly Corner' (1908).

Not Lost: 'Michelangelo' is a subway stop on the Milan Metropolitana. The poem is dedicated to Luciano and Mimia Erba, and to my daughter Giulia.

The House Guest: The epigraph is from Alice's conversation in 'Advice from a Caterpillar', the fifth chapter of *Alice in Wonderland*.

Kyoto Protocols: The epigraph is from Titania's speech in *A Midsummer Night's Dream* 2.i. 115-17. The poem was inspired by George Bush's visit to Kyoto in November 2005.

And a Name: Bob Dylan appears intentionally to mispronounce the word 'Mersey', which has a voiced 's', when talking to fans in the Adelphi Hotel in D. A. Pennebaker's *Don't Look Back*. He either associates the place with 'The quality' that 'is not strained' and 'droppeth . . . from heaven' in *The Merchant of Venice* (4.i.180-82), or gets its name wrong.

Heart & Company: The title is from an early draft of W. B. Yeats's 'The Circus Animals' Desertion'. The epigraph is from Baudelaire's

'Le Cygne'. The entire aside reads: 'la forme d'une ville / Change plus vite, hélas! que le cœur d'un mortel' [the form of a town / Changes faster, alas! than the human heart']. Liverpool was European Capital of Culture during 2008.

Lying Figures: The epigraphs are from 'Post-scriptum' in Valerio Magrelli's *Figure bifurcate* (2006): 'Divided and word-immune creatures / rise up before me, / invulnerable to the truth'; and Nelly Sach's early poem 'An euch, die das neue Haus bauen' [To those building the new house]: 'Build, when the hourglass trickles, / But don't weep the minutes away / Together with the dust / That the light conceals.'

Acknowledgements

Some of these poems, or their earlier versions, first appeared in the following publications and websites to whose editors grateful thanks are offered: *Agenda, Critical Quarterly, English, Fire, fourW, Jacket, Matrix, Metre, Moving Worlds, nd[re]view, Notre Dame Review, nth position, Poetry Ireland Review, Poetry Review, The Reader, Route 57, Salt, Shearsman, Signals, Tears in the Fence, Thumbscrew,* and *The Times Literary Supplement.*

'Calm Autumn' was published in *100 Poets against the War* ed. Todd Swift (Cambridge and Perth: Salt Publishing, 2003). 'Italian Poplars' also appeared in *80 poeti per gli ottant'anni di Luciano Erba* (Milan: Interlinar, 2003). 'Unwitting Epitaph' also appeared, with a Japanese translation by Tomoko Kurumada, in *Dialogue: Tadashi Toyama in Search of a Vessel for the Soul* (Tokyo: Itto-Henshushitsu, 2003). 'Closure', 'Stranded' and 'Italian Poplars' were first collected in *L'attaccapanni e altre poesie* trans. Ornella Trevisan and the author (Bergamo: Moretti & Vitali, 2004). 'What Lies Sleeping' was published with a Spanish version by Jaime Thonney Prunnell in *Clarin: Revista de Nueva Literatura* no. 54, Nov-Dec 2004. 'York Notes' was included in *Mairi MacInnes: A Tribute* (Nottingham: Shoestring Press, 2005). 'The Red Dusk', 'Mention in Dispatches', 'The False Perspectives', 'Frost Shadows', and 'Disorientation' also appeared in the *Warp and Weft* anthology ed. Peter Carpenter and Amanda Knight (Tonbridge: Worple Press, 2007). 'On the Mobile' was first published in *Speaking English, an anthology for John Lucas,* ed. Andy Croft (Nottingham: Five Leaves Press, 2007).

Printed in the United States
103118LV00002B/75/A

9 781905 700455